Your World

Investigating Measurement

Volume and Mass

Torrey Maloof

Consultants

Michele Ogden, Ed.D
Principal, Irvine Unified School District

Jennifer Robertson, M.A.Ed.
Teacher, Huntington Beach City School District

Publishing Credits

Rachelle Cracchiolo, M.S.Ed., *Publisher*
Conni Medina, M.A.Ed., *Managing Editor*
Dona Herweck Rice, *Series Developer*
Emily R. Smith, M.A.Ed., *Series Developer*
Diana Kenney, M.A.Ed., NBCT, *Content Director*
Stacy Monsman, M.A., *Editor*
Kevin Panter, *Graphic Designer*

Image Credits: All images from iStock and/or
Shutterstock.

Teacher Created Materials
5301 Oceanus Drive
Huntington Beach, CA 92649-1030
http://www.tcmpub.com

ISBN 978-1-4807-5807-0

Table of Contents

Mealtime Measuring

How do you measure things when you help cook dinner? Do you use cups? Do you use spoons? Do you add a pinch of something to a mixing bowl? You probably do not measure everything the same way. The way you measure things depends on the units that are needed. And before you start cooking, you need to make sure you have what you need.

When people shop for ingredients, they must make sure they buy the right amounts. Otherwise, they will not be able to follow their recipes. Luckily, most foods have labels. Those labels list key measurements. For instance, the label on a bag of rice will tell you how much rice is in the bag. The label on a bottle of water will tell you how much water is in the bottle. It is important to know what these numbers mean. Numbers are important inside and outside of the kitchen.

ORGANIC BEEF
100% GRASS-FED

Organic
Ground Beef

0122-4567

1 kilogram

SPRING WATER
NATURAL SPRING WATER
16.9 FL OZ 500 ml

RICE
PREMIUM QUALITY

NET WT. 1LB. (454g)

Original
CORN
FLAKES

original CORN

Original
Corn
Flakes

Original CORN

Nutrition Facts
Serving Size 1 medium (180g)

Amount Per Serving
Calories 32   Calories from Fat 3
                              % Daily Value*

Total Fat 0g
Saturated Fat 0g
Trans Fat
Cholesterol 0mg
Sodium 8mg
Total Carbohydrate 7g
Dietary Fiber 7g
Protein 5g

Calories
110

LET'S EXPLORE MATH

There are two boxes of the same cereal in the pantry.
The two boxes are exactly the same size. One box is
unopened and full. The other box has been opened
and some of the cereal has been eaten.

1. Which box of cereal is heavier? How do
    you know?

2. How can you find how much heavier one box
    of cereal is than the other? List your steps.

The Same Language

Can you speak more than one language? Or, do you know someone who can speak a language that you don't know? Whatever the case may be, there is one language that is known all over the world—math! Math is a **universal** language. We can use numbers to talk about the world around us.

How do numbers help us describe our world? Well, numbers are often used to describe measurements. The weight of a solid object depends on how much **matter** is in that object. That amount is called **mass**. The more mass things have, the heavier they will be. Liquids are measured differently, though. They are measured by the amount of space they take up. That amount is called **volume**.

While numbers are all the same, units vary. The **metric system** has units that can be used to talk about temperature, length, mass, and volume. It is based on the number 10. Metric units such as **kilograms** (kg) and **grams** (g) measure mass. **Liters** (L) and **milliliters** (mL) are common units used to measure volume.

A pinch of salt is less than 1 gram.

A D-battery is about 150 grams.

A drop of water is less than 1 milliliter.

A bag of apples is about 1 kilogram.

A bottle of soda is about 1 liter.

LET'S EXPLORE MATH

Which unit of measurement would be best to measure each item's mass or volume?

kilogram   gram   liter   milliliter

1. water in a fish tank
2. weight of a dollar bill
3. liquid in a tear drop
4. weight of a dictionary

Take a Good Guess

What if you don't have time to find an exact measurement? Take breakfast, for example. Do you measure the milk before pouring it into your cereal bowl? Or, do you just pour until it looks right? Chances are that you do the latter. But this is more than a guess. It's based on what you know.

The bowl holds a certain amount of liquid. The dry cereal is already taking up some room in that bowl. That information can be used to pour the right amount of milk. This is called **estimating**. If your estimate is wrong, your breakfast might not be what you hoped for.

Estimation is used every day. People estimate how long it will take to get to school or work. Shoppers estimate how much groceries will cost. These are not random guesses. They are based on information that is known.

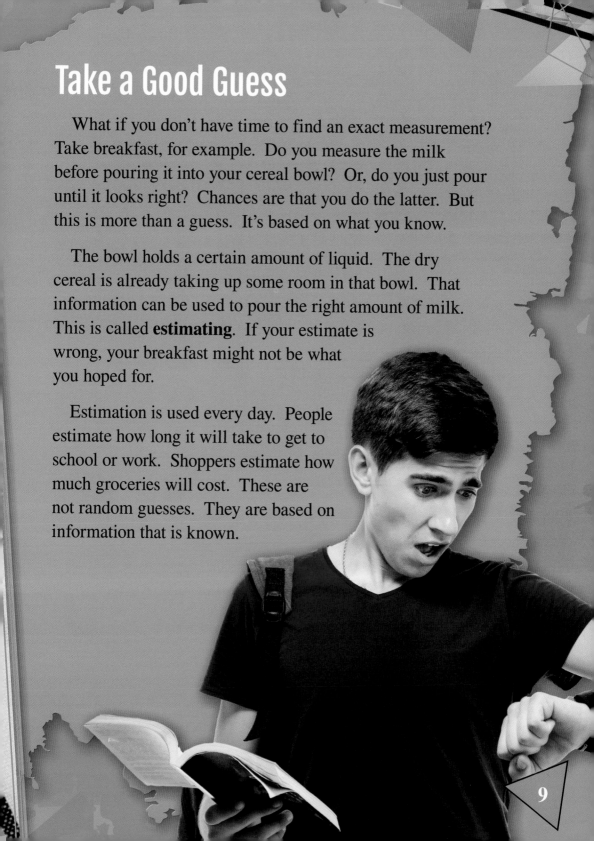

It is helpful to estimate with familiar objects. Imagine holding a large dictionary. Does it feel light? Heavy? It actually has a mass of about 1 kg. Knowing this can help you make a good guess about the mass of another object. For example, how many dictionaries would have about the same mass as a cat? If your guess is about two dictionaries, then you made a pretty good guess.

It works with volume, too. Think about a teapot. A teapot holds about 1 L of water. How many liters would it take to fill a bathroom sink? Imagine pouring water from a teapot into a sink. How many teapots would it take to fill it? If your guess is around eight full teapots, then you are getting good at this!

Two dictionaries have about the same mass as one cat.

A bathroom sink holds about eight teapots worth of water.

LET'S EXPLORE MATH

Estimate the volume of each of the items below.

less than 1 L   about 1 L   about 50 L   about 100 L

1.

3.

2.

4.

Although backpacks may cause backaches, they don't cause scoliosis, the condition seen in this X-ray.

Daily Decisions

Do you think estimating is only used in math class? Maybe you believe that measuring only happens in a science lab. Or, perhaps you think real-world math is only found in the kitchen. Think again! Estimating can help you make decisions in everyday life.

Backbreaking Backpack

Lynn loves books. She enjoys reading and likes to learn new things. Her favorite books are about history. The school librarian helps her choose a new topic each week. This week, she is reading about the pyramids in Egypt. She is learning many cool things about mummies and pharaohs. But, her love of books is causing a problem. History books can be big books!

Last week, Lynn's back started to hurt. The librarian thinks her backpack is causing the pain. She thinks it is too heavy for her. But Lynn disagrees. She estimates that her backpack has a mass of about 2 kg. The librarian estimates that Lynn's backpack has a mass of about 5 kg. She asks Lynn to measure the mass of her backpack. She wants her to share the measurement with the school nurse.

Lynn begins to empty her backpack. There is a lot of stuff! As she takes each item out, she begins to think that her estimate of 2 kg may be too low. But, she still does not think the total mass is more than 5 kg.

Lynn makes a list of the items in her backpack. Some of the items are not very heavy. She has things like pencils, a homework folder, and some money. She does not include these on the list. She knows they have a mass of only a few grams or less. But, Lynn does include her three books, her water bottle, and her laptop. She estimates the mass of each object to be about 1 kg. She adds the five items together. The total mass of her backpack is about 5 kg. The librarian was right! The nurse agrees that Lynn has too much in her backpack. Rather than ditch her books, Lynn buys a backpack with wheels. Problem solved!

Amelia is the school's best baseball player. But, her teammates think she should empty her bag more often. They think the total mass of her sports bag must be over 10,000 grams!

1. The table below lists the mass of objects in Amelia's enormous sports bag. What is the total?

Items	Total Mass
	500 g
	2,000 g
	1,500 g
	500 g
	500 g

2. Do you think the team's estimate was a good estimate? Why or why not? Explain your reasoning.

Hydrated and Healthy

At school last week, Ruby learned all about **nutrition**. A doctor talked to her class. The doctor told students about the wholesome foods they should be eating. She talked to them about exercise, too. "Healthy food and activity can make you feel good inside and out," she said. The doctor also talked about drinking water. She explained why staying **hydrated** is a good thing.

Luckily, Ruby already runs a lot. Plus, she plays on her school's soccer team. Both are great workouts! She makes good food choices, too. But there is one thing Ruby does not do—drink enough water. Ruby wants to make a change. She wants to be as healthy as possible. She has a big soccer game coming up, and she wants to be in tip-top shape. Ruby is determined to start drinking more water.

The doctor told students that they should drink 2 L of water a day. Ruby decides to put her math skills to use. She plans to make a table. The table will help her make sure she is drinking enough water each day.

Ruby knows there are 1,000 mL in 1 L. So, she must drink 2,000 mL of water each day. Ruby has two water bottles that are different sizes. She has a small green one. It holds 500 mL. She also has a big silver one. It holds 800 mL. She uses the silver one when she plays soccer because it holds more water. She gets very thirsty when she dribbles the ball up and down the field under the hot sun. Ruby thinks about the total volume of each water bottle. Then, she makes her table.

Ruby tallys each time she drinks a full bottle of water. Use her table to answer the questions below.

Days	Green Bottle (500 mL)	Silver Bottle (800 mL)
Monday	I I	I
Tuesday	I I I I	
Wednesday	I	I I
Thursday	I	I
Friday	I I I	I
Saturday		I I I
Sunday	I I	I I

1. How many milliliters of water did Ruby drink on Wednesday?

2. On which days did Ruby meet her goal of drinking 2,000 mL? On which days did she not meet her goal?

3. How many milliliters of water did Ruby drink this week?

Dog Days of Summer

Trevor's dog, Wally, has been his best friend since he was a little boy. Wally looks and acts like a teddy bear. He is loving and fluffy. He is also funny. He likes to do silly things to make Trevor laugh. One time, he rolled around in a large mud puddle for hours. When he was done, only Wally's eyes could be seen under the layers of thick mud.

Wally is always there for Trevor. And Trevor is always there for Wally. But, Trevor is going on a trip this summer. He is going to Europe with his parents. They will be gone for two weeks.

Trevor wants to make sure he leaves enough food and medicine for Wally with the dogsitter. Wally eats a certain amount of food every day. He also needs a small amount of medicine added to his water. To do this, Trevor uses a dropper. He knows that they will need to leave instructions for the dogsitter.

Trevor and Wally

Trevor works with his parents to plan how much food Wally should get each day. If Wally does not get enough food, his health will suffer. But if he eats too much, he could become overweight. His heart or skin might not be healthy. He could also get **arthritis**. Too much food could cause a lot of problems. So, Trevor wants to make sure Wally gets the right amount of food.

How much food should Wally get? Trevor does not just dump food into Wally's bowl. He uses a special scale to find its mass first. Wally must eat 200 g of food at each meal. And, Trevor feeds Wally twice a day. Now, Trevor has to figure out how much dog food to buy for Wally. There has to be enough for the two weeks that Trevor will be gone.

Trevor knows Wally will eat 200 grams of dog food at each meal.

1. How many grams of dog food does Wally eat each day? (Remember, Wally eats twice a day.)

2. How many grams of dog food will Wally eat in two weeks?

3. The dog food is sold in a bag with a mass of 5,000 grams. Will one bag be enough for two weeks?

23

Now, Trevor and his parents need to arrange for Wally to get his medicine. He has a brand-new bottle of it. But, Trevor is not sure there will be enough. He checks the label. It says that the total volume is 30 mL.

Trevor uses a dropper to give Wally his medicine. The dropper holds 1 mL of liquid. Trevor gives Wally two full droppers. That means Wally takes 2 mL of medicine each day. Trevor will be gone for two weeks. So, he multiplies 14 days by 2 mL. That is a total volume of 28 mL. Is there enough medicine? Yes, because 28 mL is less than 30 mL. Trevor's parents will not have to buy another bottle of Wally's medicine for the dogsitter.

30 mL

LET'S EXPLORE MATH

The dogsitter will need 28 mL of Wally's medicine over two weeks. The bottle's volume is 30 mL.

1. How many milliliters of medicine will be left after the two weeks are over?

2. The next time Trevor's parents buy Wally's medicine, the bottle size has changed. The new bottle has a volume of only 7 mL. How many bottles will they need to buy so Wally has a two-week supply?

Go Forth and Measure!

Now, the metric system is in your tool chest. What will you measure next? There are so many options. What is the mass of a peanut butter and jelly sandwich? Does a ham sandwich have greater mass? Do you think their masses should be measured in grams or kilograms?

Which sandwich has the most mass?

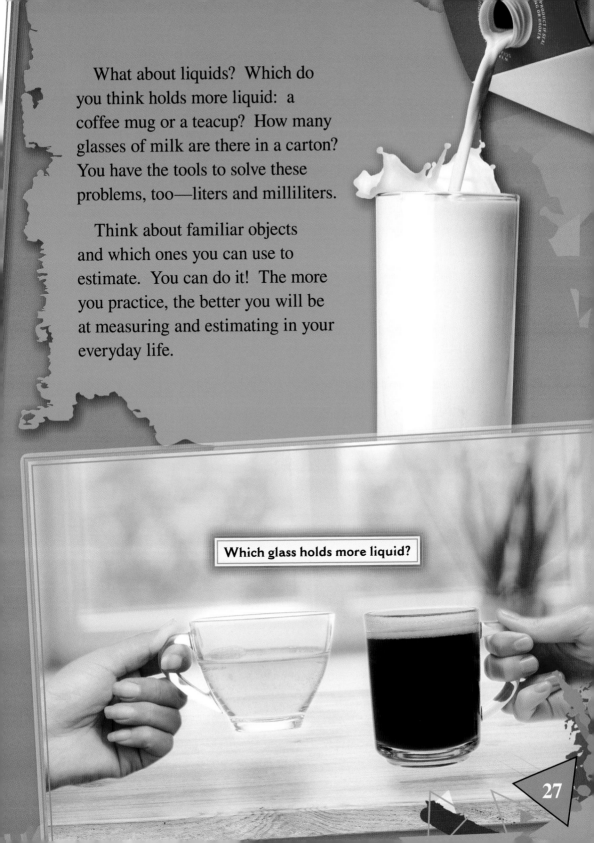

What about liquids? Which do you think holds more liquid: a coffee mug or a teacup? How many glasses of milk are there in a carton? You have the tools to solve these problems, too—liters and milliliters.

Think about familiar objects and which ones you can use to estimate. You can do it! The more you practice, the better you will be at measuring and estimating in your everyday life.

Which glass holds more liquid?

🛠 Problem Solving

Sela is going on a weekend trip with her dad. He is a pilot, and he is flying them to a campground. They will be able to hike, relax, and read. Sela is looking forward to painting some of the natural scenes. Sela's dad says that her carry-on bag cannot have a mass of more than 10 kg. Sela wants to bring a lot of stuff! She needs to plan carefully. Help Sela pack her bag.

1. Find the total mass of all of Sela's items.

2. What is the difference between the heaviest item and the lightest item?

3. List two combinations of items that Sela could pack that would keep her at or under the 10-kilogram limit. Which option would you recommend to Sela? Why?

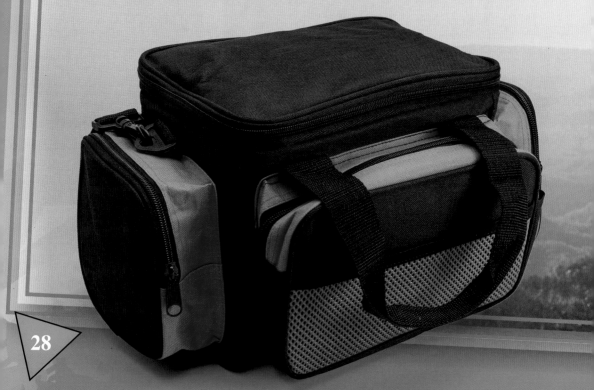

Items Sela Wants to Bring

Item	Mass
books	3 kg
hiking boots	2 kg
laptop computer	2 kg
painting supplies	4 kg
jeans	3 kg

Glossary

arthritis—a disease that causes stiffness, swelling, and soreness in joints

estimating—guessing based on observations and information

grams—metric units of mass that are equal to one thousandth of a kilogram

hydrated—having enough water

kilograms—metric units of mass that are equal to 1,000 grams

liters—metric units of volume that are equal to 1,000 milliliters

mass—the amount of matter in something

matter—anything that has mass and takes up space

metric system—a system of measures and weights that includes kilograms and liters

milliliters—metric units of volume that are equal to one thousandth of a liter

nutrition—the process of eating the right kind of food in order to be healthy

universal—the same in all places

volume—the amount of space that is filled by something

Index

31

Answer Key

Let's Explore Math

page 5:

1. The unopened box is heavier because it has more cereal in it.
2. Measure the mass of each box. Then, subtract the lighter mass from the heavier mass.

page 7:

1. Liter
2. Gram
3. Milliliter
4. Kilogram

page 11:

1. About 50 L
2. About 100 L
3. About 1 L
4. Less than 1 L

page 15:

1. 5,000 g
2. No, because the estimate is too high.

page 19:

1. 2,100 mL
2. Ruby met her goal on Tuesday, Wednesday, Friday, Saturday, and Sunday. She did not meet her goal on Monday or Thursday.
3. 14,500 mL

page 23:

1. 400 g
2. 5,600 g
3. No, one bag will not be enough for two weeks because 5,000 is less than 5,600.

page 25:

1. 2 mL
2. 4 bottles

Problem Solving

1. 14 kg
2. 2 kg
3. Answers will vary but may include: Option 1—books, laptop, easel; Option B—books, boots, laptop, jeans; Option B is better because Sela will need boots and jeans.